AMELIA EARHART

A Life from Beginning to End

Copyright © 2019 by Hourly History.

Table of Contents

Chapter One

A Turbulent Childhood

"Aviation offered such fun as crossing the continent in planes large and small, trying the whirling rotors of an autogiro, making record flights. With these activities came opportunity to know women everywhere who shared my conviction that there is so much women can do in the modern world and should be permitted to do irrespective of their sex."

—Amelia Earhart

On July 24, 1897, Amelia Mary Earhart was born in the small midwestern town of Atchison, Kansas. Atchison wasn't known for much until Amelia came along, and even today with its estimated population of just 11,000, most would have never guessed that anything of renown had come from this sleepy little town. But it was Atchison which would nurture and raise one of the most famous aviators in history, Amelia Earhart.

Amelia's father Edwin Earhart was a local attorney, and her mother was a 23-year-old debutante by the name of Amy. Following family tradition, Edwin and Amy named their firstborn daughter after their mothers, Amelia Otis and Mary Earhart. Amelia's maternal grandfather, Alfred Otis, was one of the most prominent and successful men in Atchison. He was a former judge for the United States district court as well as the bank president for Atchison Savings Bank. Taking into consideration his affluence, Alfred Otis is said to have disapproved of his daughter marrying Edwin Earhart, who came from much more humble beginnings.

Two years after Amelia's birth, she was joined by a little sister named Grace Muriel, who quickly became her childhood playmate and confidante. The two girls would both later recall that their mother was an unconventional parent at the time—teaching them to be strong and independent from a young age. This independence allowed them to avoid becoming "nice little girls," with Amelia especially shirking the overtly feminine values that most women had pressed upon them during the day and age in which the girls grew up. Amelia was known to have a streak of willful determination that was uncommon for the time. She loved to spend endless hours outside, exploring her surroundings to their fullest and collecting all manner of creatures. As a child, she is said to have had quite a collection of tree toads, katydids, worms, moths, lightning bugs, and the like.

Aside from her rough-and-tumble antics when she played outside, Amelia had a fairly routine and structured existence as a homeschooled child. The first major change in young Amelia's life came in 1907 when her father's work had him picking up shop and moving to Des Moines, Iowa. He had been working as a claims officer at a railroad company in Kansas when the decision came down to make the transfer to Des Moines. Little Amelia and her sister would not join their father and mother straight away, however; for the time being, they would remain behind in Atchison with their grandparents.

In 1909, Amelia and her sister were finally reunited with their parents, going off to live with them in Iowa. At first, their homeschooling picked up where it left off with Amelia's mother hiring a private tutor, but it was soon determined that the girls needed to go to public school. Amelia was now in the seventh grade, and despite her previously sheltered education, she took off in the public-school domain like wildfire. She quickly became known as a bright and involved student who especially loved reading.

A little bit later that year, Amelia's father would introduce her for the first time to the world of aviation. He brought Amelia to the Iowa State Fair where an airplane was displayed to the public. The first powered airplane had been flown by the Wright brothers just a few years earlier, and Amelia had never seen anything like it. But when asked if she would like to take a ride on the craft, Amelia's reaction was immediate—she informed her father that she would rather go back to the merry go round. Later, Amelia explained that she was not very impressed by the airplane, calling it "a thing of rusty wire and wood and not at all interesting."

Shortly after this adventure, Edwin Earhart received the good news that he had been promoted to become the head of the claims department. For a man who had struggled his entire life to hold down a job and secure a stable income, this was indeed exciting news. Finally feeling financially secure, the Earharts relocated to a bigger home, and Mrs. Earhart was even able to hire a maid. Even so, due to chronic excess expenditure and a failure to budget, it wasn't long before the family was running out of money. Amelia's father, meanwhile, who was now in his fifties, was suffering from terrible depression over his inadequacies when it came to providing for his family. In his despair, he started to succumb to an old vice of his— heavy drinking. Sadly, unable to face his demons, Edwin began to retreat from the family altogether.

In the midst of this turmoil, by late 1910, Amelia Earhart had already been taken back to her grandparents' home in Atchison, Kansas. At this time, her grandmother was suffering from ill health and getting progressively worse. As such, Amelia tended to her grandmother just as often as she did her schoolwork. This was a heavy burden for such a young girl, but Amelia handled it well. Her grandmother would lose her struggle a couple of years later, passing away in February of 1912. In her grandmother's will, a substantial amount of inheritance money had been left to Amelia's mother, but it carried with it a time-constraining stipulation. It dictated that the money must remain in a trust for 20 years or "until the death of Samuel Edwin Earhart."

Edwin Earhart, devastated by the obvious lack of confidence that his in-laws had in him, struggled to make ends meet. In 1915, he switched jobs once again, dragging his family with him to his latest position as a clerk for a freight office in St. Paul, Minnesota to live with him in a spacious yet rundown rental. Amelia, now a junior in high school, was enrolled at St. Paul's Central High School. At first things went well enough, but alcoholism and an inability to stay on the job continued to haunt Amelia's father. Edwin Earhart needed help, and at this point even

Amelia began to consider staging an intervention, as was evidenced on one particular occasion in which she happened to find her father's hidden stash of whiskey in his sock drawer. Seeing the hated bottle of liquor, Amelia Earhart quickly confiscated it and poured its contents down the nearest drain. Her father caught her in the act and, enraged to see his alcohol wasted, lifted his hand to strike her down. In the nick of time, Amelia's mother happened upon them and, seeing what Edwin was about to do, she grabbed her husband's hand and forced him to reconsider. The damage was already done, however, and even though her father's hand had been stayed, Amelia felt as if she had been dealt a severe blow.

Chapter Two

Finding Her Way

"Ours is the commencement of a flying age, and I am happy to have popped into existence at a period so interesting."

—Amelia Earhart

They call it the turbulent teens, but for Amelia Earhart the malevolent winds that buffeted her teenage years were a little too hard to take. The winds of fate seemed to shift on a daily basis, and depending on the fortunes of her father's faltering career, she would be inevitably sucked in by the downdraft.

In the fall of 1915, Amelia's father claimed to have been given a position by the Burlington Railroad in Springfield, Missouri, and just like that the family was expected to pack their bags and move yet again. Despite the hardship, they dutifully did what they were told and followed Edwin Earhart to Springfield, where they lived in a rundown boarding house while he lined up his job prospects. As it turns out, he was never able to land the permanent position he sought; instead, Edwin was offered a measly temp job that wouldn't be enough to support his family and certainly didn't merit the fact that he had uprooted his family and dragged them out of state.

It was at this low point that the Earhart family finally disintegrated, and Amy and Edwin went their separate ways. Amelia's father returned to Kansas to stay at his sister's house, while Amelia and her sister went with their mother to Chicago where a friend had agreed to give them a place to stay until Amelia's mother could get back on her feet. They eventually rented a home close to the University of Chicago campus. From here, Amelia attended nearby Hyde Park High School. The previously boisterous and outspoken Amelia was now finding herself quite morose and melancholy, unable to make friends. This was captured in the school's yearbook, which depicted a photo of Amelia with the caption, "A. E. (Amelia Earhart)—the girl in brown who walks alone."

Amelia had had a falling out with her peers early on in her tenure at the school. Apparently, her English class was instructed by an irresponsible teacher, who instead of teaching gave students an hour of free time and an A for the day. Most students would be overjoyed to have such a laid-back teacher, but Amelia, who was serious about her education, felt insulted. She created a petition to have the teacher fired and asked her fellow students to sign their names. As you might imagine, most of the students who rather enjoyed their free time balked at the notion and harshly ridiculed Amelia as being way too straight-laced for their tastes. Amelia, not wishing to step foot in the class again, hid in the library every single day when the hour of that particular class arrived. She was miserable. Upon her graduation in 1916, Amelia didn't even attend the ceremony with the other students. But, as disillusioned as

Amelia was with her life at this point, things were about to look up.

After Amelia's mother had received news that her brother, who had hitherto been in charge of the estate, had squandered a large chunk of their inheritance, she decided to contest the matter in court. The judge ultimately ruled that Amelia's grandmother had been incompetent when she signed the terms of the trust, and therefore the terms of the trust were nullified, and Amelia's mother was to receive the money that was due her immediately.

With this sudden influx of funds, Amelia's mother made sure to pay the tuition for Amelia to attend college at the Ogontz School for Young Ladies in Rydal, Pennsylvania. Located on what is now part of the Penn State campus, the Ogontz School required Amelia to live on campus, setting her onto the path of independence that she had secretly longed for. She arrived by train on October 3, 1916, ready to get started. Amelia enrolled under what she would later describe as the cold, hard gaze of the owner and headmistress, a woman named Abby Sutherland.

Ms. Sutherland ran a tight ship at the Ogontz School and made sure that the students under her charge did not have time to be idle. Amelia's routine was filled with classes, sports, and extracurricular activities. The school also apparently supplied a large amount of instruction in correct social behavior. In fine-tuning the students into what the school deemed to be prim and proper citizens, no stone was left unturned. Amelia wrote home to her mother describing how, on one occasion in particular, they were teaching the female students how to properly sit down in a chair: "She put a little chair out in the middle of this huge room and we all aimed at it and tried to clammer [sic] on it gracefully. It was a scream. One of the girls landed with her legs crossed, on the extreme edge. I got on but not with noticeable grace as there was no comment made."

Amelia was 19 years old at this point; she was still learning a lot about the world and was actively searching for belonging and fulfillment in life. In her younger years, Amelia often felt ignored, undervalued, and unnoticed, but at Ogontz, she found her place. Even Ms. Sutherland developed a soft spot for Amelia, writing to her mother that Amelia's "charm of manner has made a warm place for herself in the hearts of schoolmates and teachers."

Chapter Three

Breaking Records

"I have often been asked what I think about at the moment of take-off. Of course, no pilot sits and feels his pulse as he flies. He has to be part of the machine. If he thinks of anything but the task in hand, then trouble is probably just around the corner."

—Amelia Earhart

As the year 1917 came to a close, Amelia Earhart had a lot on her mind. The world stage had already been set ablaze by World War I, and American entry into the fray had affected every aspect of civilian life. Amelia had contributed to the war effort during the first phase of American participation by knitting socks and sweaters for the troops in a special program sponsored by the Red Cross.

But the real toll of war would not hit home for her until she spent Christmas in Toronto, Canada, where her sister was enrolled at St. Margaret's College. Amelia would later recall walking through the busy streets of this Canadian city and seeing wounded soldiers just back from the war, walking on crutches. The sight of the amputated soldiers stirred something in Amelia's heart and made her realize that she wanted to do more to help these young men than knitting sweaters. A week later, Amelia decided that she would leave school to work as a nursing assistant. Her help was certainly needed since at the time it is said that in Canada alone, standard hospitals that normally held 2,500 beds were accommodating more than 12,000 beds.

Thus, in April of 1918, Amelia Earhart began work at Toronto's Spadina Military Hospital where she saw to the health of veterans fresh from combat suffering from all manner of injuries. As a sad legacy of the widespread chemical warfare of World War I, many of these men suffered from what Amelia termed "ailments of the chest." In other words, their breathing capacity had been severely diminished from inhaling the fumes of lethal chemical weapons.

Amelia is said to have taken her job at the hospital very seriously and worked some very long shifts when she was able to. Despite the heavy workload, she also took time to see the sights of Toronto with her sister Muriel. Amelia found time to play tennis, enjoy horse riding, and even watched a few of the city's famous hockey matches. It was when she was riding horses that she made the acquaintance of three pilots from the RCAF (Royal Canadian Air Force). After Amelia and her sister struck up a friendship with the men, they were invited to the military airfield to watch the planes fly. Amelia was immediately fascinated by the sight.

Not long after, she went to an air show at the Canadian National Exposition grounds. Unlike the rickety old biplane that she had seen with her father all those years ago, here Amelia saw some really impressive aircraft with equally impressive pilots. Even when one daring (and some would say reckless) pilot began to fly exceptionally low to the ground to frighten and excite the crowd below, Amelia didn't even flinch while the rest of the crowd scattered. She stood her ground and stared up at the sight with true wonder and exhilaration. The freedom of flight expressed by this daredevil pilot would leave an impression on Amelia for the rest of her life. But for the time being, she would have to return to the daily grind.

After this outing, Amelia went back to her long shifts at the hospital. The swelling ranks of her veteran patients did not begin to subside until the close of World War I on November 11, 1918. Amelia Earhart would later recall the theatrics present in the streets of Toronto when the war was declared over. She saw people dancing in the street, flags raised and bonfires lit. Amelia, thinking of the crippled, mangled men she cared for in the veterans' ward, was not much in the mood for celebration. She would later remark of the event that there was not one "serious word of thanksgiving in all that hullabaloo." Amelia now knew first hand the real cost of war, and to her—no matter how big the celebration was afterward—war did not at all seem worth the cost.

The following year, Amelia returned to the United States where she began attending classes at Columbia University in New York for a premedical program. Here she rented a room and lived communally with several other students. By all accounts, she enjoyed her time at Columbia and seemed to make a lot of friends there. Amelia completed only one year at the school, however, before deciding to quit and leave New York for the West Coast. Her parents had managed to come to terms and, ending their separation, moved into a home together in Los

Angeles, California. Edwin Earhart had supposedly sobered up and even found work practicing law.

Despite previous disappointments, Amelia was willing to give her father a chance. In the summer of 1920, she joined her parents in Los Angeles. One of the early highlights of her return to family life was an air show at an airfield in Long Beach, which Amelia went to with her father. It was during this show that she first expressed an interest in flying aboard a plane herself. Edwin Earhart, always happy to oblige his daughter, took Amelia to an airfield a few days later and bought the ticket required for a ride. Amelia was immediately hooked, and the craft had barely left the ground before she had made up her mind: "I knew I myself had to fly."

Looking into the matter further, Amelia came across 24-year-old Neta Snook. Only one year older than Amelia, Neta was a pioneering young pilot eager to take on an enterprising student such as Amelia. Amelia paid for her lessons with Neta through money she had saved up while working as a file clerk for a local telephone company.

In early January of 1921, Amelia boarded Neta's dual-controlled Canuck for the first time. Neta started slowly with Amelia, showing her the basic controls of the craft and teaching her how to taxi on the ground. From there, Amelia rapidly progressed. She proved to be an extraordinarily quick study, and it wasn't long before she was taking her first flight. After only a few more hours spent in the air, Amelia was already considered a capable and experienced pilot.

But merely flying wasn't enough for Amelia—she wanted to own her own plane. Aided by her mother, she managed to achieve this feat by working several part-time jobs and saving as much of her paychecks as she could until her dream of airplane ownership was realized in the summer of 1922. Once she had a plane of her own, Amelia spent just about every weekend flying or going to air shows. Flying was her life, and she was soon a regular at the air shows and rodeos, where she performed as a featured flyer.

Inspired by her success at air shows, Amelia set a new goal for herself: she wanted to break the altitude record for female pilots. Sure enough, on October 22, 1922, Earhart soared above 14,000 feet, making a name for herself as the highest-flying female pilot to date.

Chapter Four

First Transatlantic Flight

"Among all the marvels of modern invention, that with which I am most concerned is, of course, air transportation. Flying is perhaps the most dramatic of recent scientific attainment. In the brief span of thirty odd years, the world has seen an inventor's dream first materialized by the Wright brothers at Kitty Hawk become an everyday actuality."

—Amelia Earhart

Amelia Earhart officially received her pilot's license on May 15, 1923. Her license listed her as an official aviator pilot, the sixteenth woman in the world to achieve this honor. Even though Amelia had not yet fully entertained the notion that she would spend the rest of her life flying, for the moment she was quite satisfied with her accomplishments. This bit of happiness would serve as a vital cushion for the turbulence that Amelia's family would once again cause in her life.

After separating and getting back together, Amelia's parents would finally file for divorce in 1924. This was the final stroke that brought to an end a marriage that could occasionally be idyllic, but more often than not was far from ideal. After Amelia's father departed, it wasn't long before Amelia's mother realized that she needed a fresh start. Wishing to move as far from California as she could, she suggested to Amelia that they should move to Boston to join Amelia's sister Muriel, who had enrolled for classes there as a university student.

Amelia agreed. She even decided to sell her precious plane (which she had dubbed the *Canary* because of its bright yellow color) to be able to purchase a car so that she and her mother could make the drive to Boston. This may seem like a drastic decision to make, but Amelia was apparently willing to make it. One strange consequence of Amelia's sale of the plane was that the young man who purchased it from her crashed it during his very first flight, killing himself and his passenger. Although this disturbingly tragic accident shook Earhart, she rationalized the event as being the result of a pilot who was overconfident and who made unnecessary mistakes.

At any rate, after the sale of her plane, Amelia used the money to buy a 1922 Kissel Kar. She loved the car, with its yellow paint job, prominent headlights, and convertible top. It was with this vehicle that she took her mother on the road, driving across the country all the way to New England. The trip itself would take six weeks but could have been achieved much sooner if it wasn't for Amelia's determination to make the most of the journey. She made frequent stops along the way to sightsee in places such as Yosemite and Sequoia National Park. At one point she even took her mother to Alberta, Canada in order to see the sprawling Canadian countryside.

Once they reached their final destination, Amelia's mother signed a lease for a rental home, and Amelia tried to get used to her new surroundings of suburban Boston. She would not be there for long, however, because her mother soon agreed to pay the tuition for Amelia to go back to Columbia University in New York. Amelia enrolled once again at her old stomping grounds of Columbia University in September of 1924. She was going to make a go of it again as a college student, but the effort would not last for very long.

By early 1925, Amelia's mother was having significant enough financial trouble that Amelia had to drop out the next semester. Taking it upon herself to get a job to help support them both, Amelia found work at Denison House, a program that aided Boston's growing immigrant population. Here she taught immigrant children English and served as a kind of social worker for their families. Just as was the case when she tended wounded troops as a nursing assistant, Amelia in many ways felt her best when she was helping others.

It wouldn't be long before the thrill of flight would once again come calling. Amelia sought entry and was accepted into Boston's local branch of the National Aeronautic Association. Now that she had been welcomed back into the fold of aeronautics, she just needed to get her hands on a new plane. The opportunity presented itself when Bert Kinner, the man who had built Amelia's *Canary*, gave Amelia a plane to fly for demonstrations at the nearby Dennison airport. This partnership would continue to expand with Amelia becoming an official sales rep for the company and even a stockholder.

Amelia's next pivotal moment in her life occurred on May 21, 1927, when she heard that famed pilot Charles Lindbergh had flown solo directly from New York to

Paris—the first pilot ever to have done so. Earhart was amazed at both Lindbergh's daring flight and the huge fanfare that resulted from it. Lindbergh was an overnight superstar, and Amelia, the quiet often overlooked girl from Kansas, wished that she too could bask in some of that glory. She was now nearly 30 years old and wondered just how much farther her life as a pilot would take her. Her answer to this question seemed to come by way of a phone call she received in April of 1928.

On the other end of the phone was a man named Hilton H. Railey. Railey was inquiring for a publishing company in New York called G. P. Putnam's Sons that wished to bring Amelia on board for an airborne publicity stunt similar in nature to Charles Lindbergh's transatlantic flight. Unlike Lindbergh's solo mission, this flight would have Earhart as part of a team with a pilot named Wilmer Stultz at the helm, as well as a mechanic named Louis Gordon on board.

The plane holding this crew, aptly named *Friendship*, took flight on June 3, 1928, sending Amelia and her cohorts into the skies. Shortly after take-off, the plane stopped briefly in Newfoundland where it was fueled and prepped for the main flight across the Atlantic. While doing so, however, meteorological conditions worsened dramatically, causing the flight across the Atlantic to be postponed for two whole weeks.

Amelia and the crew were all incredibly anxious by the time their day of departure arrived on June 17. It was initially difficult to lift the heavy plane into the air, and precious extra fuel had to be offloaded in order to lighten the plane's weight enough to get airborne. Nevertheless, the plane was eventually able to rise up and begin its crossing, barreling through the skies toward the European continent. Some 20 hours later, *Friendship* and its crew landed in Wales at the airfield in Burry Port. The crossing itself broke records, and the fact that Amelia was on board made her the very first woman to have successfully crossed the Atlantic by plane.

After this feat, Amelia Earhart was, for all intents and purposes, quite famous, but you wouldn't know it from her initial reception. Emerging off-course from their intended landing site, the crew of *Friendship* had to depend upon the kindness of strangers to pull them to shore. The first person they encountered was Norman Fisher, the high sheriff of Carmarthenshire, who sailed across the waters in a small dinghy next to the big seaplane. When he made eye contact with Amelia as she poked her head out of the hatch, Norman asked rather bluntly, "Do ye be wanting something?" To which Amelia quickly responded, "We've come from America—where are we?" The man duly informed her, "Well, I'm sure we wish you welcome to Burry Port Wales. I'll see about getting ye mooring space for the flying machine and getting ye ashore." True to his word, Norman then secured aid to bring Amelia and her crewmates to shore. Shortly thereafter, those in Britain who were eagerly waiting for Amelia's arrival were alerted to the news and kicked off an extravagant welcome party.

After all the fanfare had subsided, the crew boarded a boat and set sail back across the Atlantic from which they had come. Upon her return to the United States, Amelia Earhart was certainly not idle—now instantly recognizable, she toured the country with her crewmates, Gordon and

Stultz. Everybody wanted a chance to congratulate Amelia, give her flowers, or ask her autograph. Before the year was out, G. P. Putnam's Sons published Earhart's story of the transatlantic flight in the form of a book entitled *20 Hours, 40 Min: Our Flight in the Friendship*.

In March 1929, Amelia saw yet another milestone when she passed her exams for obtaining a transport pilot license—the fourth woman in the world to do so. Later that summer, she was hired on at Transcontinental Air Transport as a kind of official sponsor. Here she was often tasked with promoting the safety of air travel to women. By this point, Amelia had acquired enough resources to buy a new plane. Her new ride, a Lockheed Vega, was much faster than any of the previous planes she had flown. Fittingly, the very same day that she became the official owner of the Vega, Amelia entered herself into an all-female air race.

Out of a group of nineteen fliers, Amelia Earhart managed to finish in third place after only having piloted her plane a few times. This was then followed by an effort on Amelia's part to break the speed record for female pilots. She promptly set three new records by July 5, 1930. As it turns out, these efforts were being encouraged by George Putnam of G. P. Putnam's Sons, who was in charge of Amelia's publicity and made sure she remained in the limelight.

Soon Earhart was working with companies seeking to profit from the nascent yet quickly expanding airline industry of the 1930s. Amelia quickly rose through the ranks of Transcontinental Air Transport and became the vice-president of public relations. This role kept her busy as she would make many public appearances and give lengthy speeches on the subject of air travel. As a result of all this publicity, Amelia Earhart soon became a household name in the United States. People admired her rugged individualism and free-spirited nature. Amelia Earhart essentially became a symbol of the things that Americans hold most dear.

Chapter Five

Earhart in the White House

"Mostly, my flying has been solo, but the preparation for it wasn't. Without my husband's help and encouragement, I could not have attempted what I have. Ours has been a contented and reasonable partnership, he with his solo jobs and I with mine. But always with work and play together, conducted under a satisfactory system of dual control."

—Amelia Earhart

Amelia's publicist, George Putnam—or as his friends liked to call him, G. P.—had Amelia taking on one speaking engagement or promo after another. Putnam was intensely interested in Earhart and her rise to prominence, and some began to wonder if this interest went beyond business relations. G. P.'s wife Dorothy, for one, had her suspicions. As her husband drifted away from her and toward Amelia, she decided to go ahead and file for divorce on December 19, 1929. It remains uncertain just how close George and Amelia were prior to the divorce, but at any rate, they certainly didn't waste any time in finalizing their own personal partnership by becoming wed on February 7, 1931.

Amelia was 33 years old at the time of the wedding, and George Putnam was a decade her senior at 43. Some have argued that the union of Putnam and Earhart was more of a strategic partnership than true love since both were so actively involved in the promotion of aviation. Earhart was a true progressive and a career woman before the concept had even been fully conceived. In that sense, it certainly was convenient for her to be married to a man who was a publicist and could promote her and her efforts like no other. In truth, there were other pilots of Amelia's caliber at the time, but with Putnam's help, Earhart had become the most famous female pilot of the 1930s. People not only loved her flying ability, but as she was seen in commercials and promotional material a strong affection grew for her good looks, witty style, and even her fashion sense. Indeed, Macy's even started selling a clothing line designed by Amelia.

Despite the rampant commercialization of her image, Earhart was the real deal when it came to flight—and especially testing out new aircraft, which was evidenced when she was chosen to be the test pilot of a so-called autogyro, a craft that was a forerunner of what would become the modern helicopter. Earhart, always a quick study, was able to learn the controls of the craft in a relatively short period of time. After mastering the craft, she was able to take it up to over 18,415 feet. This was then followed by a flight from Newark, New Jersey all the way to Oakland, California. Amelia's husband George was sure to put out several publications documenting the voyage along the way.

But this trip would be nothing compared to what Amelia planned next—a solo trip across the Atlantic. Amelia scoffed at her previous transatlantic trip with a three-person crew as being nothing more than her being brought along like a sack of potatoes, but now she was going to be the only pilot on board, flying from coast to coast by herself. The biggest hurdle that Amelia had to overcome to do so was her aversion to looking at onboard instruments while flying. Up until this point, Amelia had simply used maps and her own two eyes to chart where to fly and where to land, but this would not be possible when flying over the immense Atlantic Ocean. To accurately navigate her flight, Amelia absolutely had to learn how to use the complicated control panels of her cockpit.

As such, she spent several months getting herself acquainted with all the controls on her plane. It wasn't until May 20, 1932 that Amelia decided she was ready. Fittingly, exactly five years earlier, Charles Lindbergh had set out on the very first solo transatlantic flight. The stage was set perfectly; it was time for Amelia Earhart to earn her stripes. Just as evening fell, she soared off the runway in Harbor Grace, Newfoundland to begin her flight across the Atlantic. Only four hours into the fourteen-hour flight, the weather took a turn for the worse, and Amelia ran into a severe storm which would make the rest of her journey a fight for her life. The plane was being dangerously weighed down by ice, and many of the vital instruments Amelia needed to navigate her way across the ocean malfunctioned due to the terrible weather conditions. She could no longer see at what altitude she was flying nor at what speed. Gas fumes were leaking into the cabin, and Amelia could feel drops of gasoline from the broken reserve tank drip down her neck. She could only hope that there would be enough fuel left to last her to shore—if indeed she was able to find the shore without her instruments.

Although she was way off course and nearly missed the northern-most point of Northern Ireland, Amelia managed to find her way to the coast and land in Londonderry on May 21, 1932, thereby sealing her fate as the first woman ever to have made a solo flight across the Atlantic. As before, she was met with much praise and fanfare—now even more so since she had undeniably proven herself as a capable pilot. Immensely pleased, George Putnam joined his wife in some of the celebrations. Among those sending their congratulations was Eleanor Roosevelt and her husband Franklin, the governor of New York. Franklin D. Roosevelt was at the time running for president and once elected would go on to serve longer than any other American president in history. Soon Amelia and her husband George were wining and dining with the president-elect, even attending FDR's eventual inauguration in 1933.

By the early 1930s, Amelia Earhart was already becoming well acquainted with all the celebrities and prominent people of her time, but it was the relationship with President Roosevelt and the First Lady that would be of the most consequence. As FDR began his first term in the White House, the Pentagon's eyes were already on Japan. Amelia, too, turned her attention away from the Atlantic and to the Pacific, eager to face new challenges.

Chapter Six

Attempting to Circumnavigate the Globe

"The time to worry is three months before a flight. Decide then whether or not the goal is worth the risks involved. If it is, stop worrying. To worry is to add another hazard."

—Amelia Earhart

As the year 1933 came to a close, 36-year-old Amelia Earhart had achieved much but was always looking to add even more impressive feats to her resume. When in early 1934, a group of Hawaiian aviation enthusiasts put out the word that they would pay $10,000 to the first pilot (man or woman) that could fly solo nonstop from Hawaii to America's western seaboard, Amelia was all ears. Aiding her in this task was a pilot and engineer named Paul Mantz whom she had hired to give her trusted Vega a complete service and overhaul. Once her plane was in tip-top condition, Amelia made her way to Honolulu to prepare for take-off.

On January 11, 1935, she set off, setting her sights on Oakland, California. After a grueling 18-hour flight, she landed safely in front of a crowd of 10,000 excited people. This record-setting voyage across the Pacific was followed by another solo long-distance flight from Los Angeles to

Mexico City, and then the even longer trip of Mexico City to New Jersey. At this point, Amelia felt she had pushed her Vega to the limit; she needed a new plane. She wanted a craft that could fly higher and faster, and on July 21, 1936, she got behind the controls for the first time of a Lockheed Electra that promised to do just that. After testing the plane out, Amelia decided that this sleeker, faster plane was just what she was looking for. Three days later, on what happened to be her 39th birthday, she acquired the craft. Shortly after this acquisition, Amelia found a good opportunity to break in the new plane by way of the 1936 New York to Los Angeles Bendix Air Race.

Amelia was quite used to long-distance flights at this point, but she wasn't always the best competitor when it came to battling speed pilots, a fact made obvious by her finishing fifth in the race. Still, Amelia won $500 in prize money, and she was able to use the experience to get to know her new plane. Besides, she was thinking of bigger things than simply outracing other flyers. It was shortly after this race that Amelia began to make serious plans for an attempt at circumnavigating the globe, or as Amelia put it, flying "as near its waistline as could be." There was quite a bit of planning involved in such a monumental feat—the most important of which was where Amelia Earhart would be able to effectively refuel. She would need to stop somewhere in the Pacific during the course of the flight to refuel the plane and rest before continuing on. It was determined that this pitstop would take place on the lonely, deserted Howland Island some 1,900 miles from Hawaii, right in the middle of the Pacific Ocean.

Being able to land on this island would be akin to finding a needle in a haystack, and Amelia—the pilot who enjoyed flying by the seat of her pants—would need to rely upon much more complex tools of navigation. To aid her in this task, Amelia and her husband recruited a navigation expert by the name of Fred Noonan. Noonan, who had previously worked for the budding Pan American airlines, would accompany Amelia on the flight, helping her to interpret the dials and controls that blanketed the ship's dash. Amelia would also be accompanied by Harry Manning as second navigator and Paul Mantz as co-pilot.

On March 17, 1937, Amelia and her crew set off on the first leg of their journey, flying from Oakland, California to Honolulu, Hawaii. The plane was having some technical issues during the flight, and shortly after their arrival, it was determined that it would need servicing. Upon closer inspection, it became apparent that some pretty severe problems with the plane's propellers needed to be looked into. Desiring more advanced expertise for the job, the crew decided to take the plane to the Hawaiian naval installation of Luke Field in Pearl Harbor. After the craft was serviced, Amelia and company were set to take off a few days later but ran into a snag when the plane's landing gear collapsed just before take-off. This caused the plane's propellers to slam into the pavement as the craft careened across the runway with sparks flying in every direction. This resulted in massive damage to the craft and caused the flight to be put off indefinitely until the plane could be repaired.

What was left of Amelia Earhart's Electra was then loaded up by the Army Air Corps and delivered across thousands of miles of ocean water to the Lockheed facility in Burbank, California whence it had been created. The bill that Lockheed gave Amelia was far more than either her or her husband could afford at the time, so George Putnam turned once again to his wealthy friends to see if he could raise the money for repairs. Putnam, always keen to keep a few wealthy, well-connected friends around, was ultimately successful in his fundraising, and Lockheed was instructed to proceed with their restoration of the craft. Earhart meanwhile was preparing once again to achieve the goal of a lifetime: the circumnavigation of the globe.

Chapter Seven

Amelia's Last Words

"Please know that I am aware of the hazards. I want to do it because I want to do it. Women must try to do things as men have tried. When they fail, their failure must be a challenge to others."

—Amelia Earhart

In the summer of 1937, after the Electra had been duly restored, Amelia Earhart was eager to get back into the skies. In preparation for her attempt to circumnavigate the globe, she had been quoted as saying, "I have a feeling that there is just about one more good flight left in my system, and I hope this trip is it." As usual for Amelia Earhart, it was all or nothing, and she was rearing to go.

It was on June 1, 1937 that she and Fred Noonan took to the skies from an airfield in Miami and launched into the first leg of Amelia's epic journey. Along the way, the pair made several pitstops in parts of South America, Africa, and even India before reaching the Papua New Guinean city of Lae on June 29. Reaching Lae was a major milestone, marking the completion of some 22,000 miles of Amelia Earhart's effort to circumnavigate the globe. Earhart and Noonan would stay on at Lae until early July. After making sure their plane was properly refueled, serviced, and running in optimal condition, the pair hit the runway once again on July 2, lifting off from Lae Airfield. Their next destination was to be Howland Island, an island so small—at just 1,600 feet across—it was quite easy to miss from 10,000 feet up in the air, requiring the most careful and precise efforts in navigation.

The craft is said to have left with some 1,100 gallons of fuel. This would have been just enough to reach Howland Island, with a little extra to spare in case of delays, headwind, or having to change direction upon landing. Anything taxing the plane's fuel tanks more than this extra allotment could prove fatal, so Amelia and Noonan were sure to conserve as much fuel as they possibly could.

After the pair took off from Lae, it remains unclear exactly what went on in the cockpit. The next anyone heard from Amelia and her navigator was a radio transmission received by the U.S. Coastguard vessel *Itasca*, which had been positioned near Howland Island. The crew of *Itasca* first heard Earhart's voice over the airwaves in the early morning hours of July 2, reporting the weather conditions. She stated to the listening sailors, "Cloudy weather, cloudy." They next heard from Amelia at 6:14 AM when she informed them that she was 200 miles away and requested that the *Itasca* provide bearings.

The *Itasca* sent transmission after transmission, but although they could hear Earhart—who at this point was whistling into the receiver so the *Itasca* could get a lock on her—Earhart could not hear any transmissions coming from the ship. As you can imagine, the crew of the *Itasca* were becoming quite frantic in their helplessness. In the midst of their anxiety, they once again heard Earhart chime in at 7:42 AM, informing them, "We must be on you, but we cannot see you. Fuel is running low. Been unable to reach you by radio. We are flying at 1,000 feet." At this point, things were no doubt becoming uneasy in the cockpit as Amelia Earhart and Fred Noonan realized that they were in serious trouble.

As the crew of the *Itasca* struggled to figure out what to do next, they heard Amelia on the airwaves one last time at 8:44 AM as she remarked, "We are running north and south." It was a simple navigational observation most likely indicating that Amelia and Noonan were flying in a search pattern to try to locate Howland Island, but these words would have extra significance because they would prove to be the very last known words of Amelia Earhart.

Chapter Eight

Amelia Earhart's Disappearance

"When I go, I would like to go in my plane. Quickly."

—Amelia Earhart

Just one hour after Amelia Earhart's final transmission, the U.S. Coastguard ship *Itasca* began an extensive search for the Electra in the waters surrounding Howland Island. They were soon joined with craft from the U.S. Navy, and over the next few days they scoured the entire region for any signs of Amelia Earhart, Fred Noonan, or the wreckage of their downed aircraft.

After searching the surrounding waters, the rescue team made their way to the nearby Phoenix Islands, just to the south of Howland Island in case Amelia and Fred had crash-landed there. These efforts included a navy plane that flew over the region and zeroed in particularly on Gardner Island. The island had been deserted for several decades, yet the pilot was certain that he saw recent signs of life, or as it was reported, "Here signs of recent habitation were clearly visible but repeated circling and zooming failed to elicit any answering wave from possible inhabitants and it was finally taken for granted that none were there." The report then went on to state, "At the western end of the island a tramp steamer lay high and almost dry head onto the coral beach with her back broken in two places. The lagoon at Gardner looked sufficiently deep and certainly large enough so that a seaplane or even an airboat could have landed or taken off in any direction with little if any difficulty. Given a chance, it is believed that Miss Earhart could have landed her aircraft in this lagoon and swum or waded ashore."

Although vague in nature, this was perhaps the most significant finding of the entire search which after several days had otherwise turned up nothing. With no further clue as to what had happened to Amelia Earhart or her companion, the search was called off on July 19. The search had cost a few million dollars, which was indeed considered a small fortune back in 1937. Amelia's husband George Putnam meanwhile began his own personal investigation into the disappearance.

Making use of a couple of boats, he paid a local investigator to patrol several of the nearby islands. George then directed another search of the Phoenix Islands, as well as the Gilbert and Marshall Islands. Unfortunately, these searches proved fruitless as well. Realizing that Amelia most likely would not be found, George Putnam then made legal arrangements for his wife to be declared dead. It is unclear whether George really believed all hope was gone, but regardless, he figured doing so would be the best means of being able to have himself made the steward of Amelia Earhart's estate. George Putnam was ultimately successful in his efforts, and after the legal wrangling had run its course through the courts, Amelia Earhart—daredevil, adventurer, and pilot extraordinaire—was declared legally dead on January 5, 1939.

Chapter Nine

Theories and Explanations

*"The more one does and sees and feels, the more one is
able to do, and the more genuine may be one's
appreciation of fundamental things like home, and love,
and understanding companionship."*

—Amelia Earhart

Amelia Earhart may have been declared dead some 80
years ago, but that has not stopped the rampant theories and
speculations about what exactly happened to her. The
simplest explanation would be that she flew off course,
crashed into the sea, and the wreckage was lost in the wide
expanse of the Pacific Ocean. But many other
explanations—usually with very little evidence—have been
offered over the years. Harkening all the way back to the
initial search and rescue in which recent habitation had
allegedly been discovered on the remote beaches of
Gardner Island, the idea that Amelia did indeed shipwreck
on Gardner has long been widely speculated.

It has been suggested that since Amelia couldn't
properly locate Howland Island and was unable to hear
incoming transmissions on her radio, she changed course
and headed southward where she knew other nearby islands
would be. It was believed that this southerly course would
have taken Earhart and Noonan to the Phoenix Islands, and

eventually to Gardner Island. Here it is theorized that she and Noonan attempted to survive on the lonely deserted island, but if this was the case, it seems they did not last very long. According to some theorists, Amelia Earhart's remains were actually discovered on Gardner Island back in April of 1940.

It was that year that Gerald Gallagher, a British officer of the Colonial Administrative Service, led an expedition to the Phoenix Islands during which they came upon clear signs of human habitation on Gardner Island. They found human remains, a sextant box, and a pair of shoes as well as a bottle of Benedictine. The latter of which is important because Benedictine was a type of herbal liqueur that Amelia regularly consumed. It was her favorite drink, and she was believed to have one just like it among her supplies and possessions on the Electra. Also telling is the sextant box that many have posited to be the navigator Fred Noonan's.

In the initial report, Gallagher insisted that some of the remains belonged to a woman, and that there was a chance, as he put it, "that this may be remains of Amelia Earhart." This choice of wording would ignite the fires of conspiracy theorists for decades, but after the bones were taken to Fiji and analyzed by a British lab, an official report was made that the bones belonged to a male. Things took a turn once again in 1998 when a group of forensic anthropologists took a look at the old findings and came to the conclusion that the bones did indeed belong to a female. Not only that—they were certain that the bones matched up perfectly with Amelia's profile and physical description. The actual bones themselves had long been lost, but based upon the measurements that had been taken, this group stated that they were indicative of a "tall white female of northern European ancestry." This determination would become challenged in 2015 when another group of researchers examined both reports and came to the conclusion that the initial results produced by the British in 1940 outclassed the 1998 results, and the bones were indeed that of a "middle-aged man" and most certainly "not Amelia Earhart."

This debunked theory gave way to another one that gained in popularity in recent years—the idea that the Japanese government was somehow involved in Earhart's disappearance. Although the context of the narrative has shifted over time, it has long been speculated that Amelia Earhart was captured by the Japanese. Several decades after Earhart's disappearance, an elderly woman from Saipan came forward and claimed to have seen both Amelia Earhart and Fred Noonan in Japanese custody as prisoners. Even more disturbing, she claimed that as a little girl in Saipan, she witnessed Japanese soldiers execute Amelia Earhart. She described this ill-fated woman to be dressed just like Amelia, with short hair and the same kind of flight suit. She claimed the Japanese had summarily executed Amelia on the spot by decapitation.

This tale is indeed a riveting and disturbing one, but no corroborating evidence has been discovered. Furthermore, it flies in the face of facts. Although Japan had already made some aggressive moves in China and other Asian nations, the U.S. and Japan were still on friendly terms at the time of Amelia Earhart's disappearance. In fact, when Japanese officials heard that the famed aviator had gone missing, they immediately offered to be of assistance. Japan helped in the search and rescue operations and even allowed American ships access to previously off-limits Japanese territory in their search.

Still, the theory that Amelia Earhart was held prisoner by the Empire of Japan is one that is hard to shake. As recently as 2017, several books and documentaries were made over an old photo that surfaced which featured a woman resembling Amelia Earhart and a man who looked like Fred Noonan standing at a dock at Jaluit Atoll in the Marshall Islands. The photograph was suggested to have been taken around the time of Amelia's disappearance. The contention that the two people in the photo are Earhart and Noonan has since been completely discredited, however, when it was discovered that the original copy of the photo was taken from a Japanese Travel Guide published in 1935, two years before Amelia's last flight.

But no matter how many theories may be discredited and debunked, the question remains—what happened to Amelia Earhart?

Conclusion

Over 80 years have passed since Amelia Earhart took her last flight, yet that smiling face peering out from the cockpit still haunts our collective memory. She had accomplished so much and was poised to achieve even more if the fates had only allowed her to do so. Amelia Earhart was an icon and a trendsetter in her day, but since her disappearance she transformed into something else entirely.

This feminist hero lives on as a role model, inspiring women and men alike to meet challenges head-on and to chart their own course in life. The mystery of her disappearance has only served to solidify Earhart's place in the annals of history, and efforts to find out what happened during her last ill-fated flight have not been abandoned. Robert Ballard, the man who discovered the wreck of the *Titanic*, is one of the most recent explorers to take on the challenge of locating Amelia Earhart's plane. We have yet to see if the questions surrounding Amelia Earhart's death will be answered.

Made in the USA
Middletown, DE
14 March 2020

86328603R00024